WHO'S AFRAID OF HELEN OF TROY

An Essay on Love

WHO'S AFRAID OF HELEN OF TROY

An Essay on Love

DAVID LAZAR

etruscan press

Etruscan Press
Wilkes University
84 West South Street
Wilkes-Barre, PA 18766
(570) 408-4546

WILKES UNIVERSITY

www.etruscanpress.org

Published 2016 by Etruscan Press
Printed in the United States of America
Cover design by L. Elizabeth Powers
Interior design and typesetting by Julianne Popovec
The text of this book is set in Maiola.

First Edition

16 17 18 19 5 4 3 2 1

Library of Congress Cataloguing-in-Publication Data

Lazar, David, 1957-
  Who's afraid of Helen of Troy : an essay on love / David Lazar. -- First Edition.
     pages ; cm
  ISBN 978-0-9903221-1-5
  I. Title. II. Title: Who is afraid of Helen of Troy.
  PS3612.A973 W48 2016
  814'.6--dc23
                              2015026929

Please turn to the back of this book for a list of the sustaining funders of Etruscan Press.

This book is printed on recycled, acid-free paper.

Hunger is insolent, and will be fed . . .

Odyssey, Book 7, line 100
Trans. Alex. Pope

WHO'S AFRAID OF HELEN OF TROY: AN ESSAY ON LOVE

Contents

Thanks to: Martin McGovern, Heather Frise, Adrianne Kalfopoulou, Delmore Lazar, Celeste Wiser, Stephen Sondheim, Lorenz Hart, Dorothy Fields, Cole Porter, Stephin Merritt.

WHO'S AFRAID OF HELEN OF TROY

An Essay on Love

At a Diner Near Thebes

Self-blinded like what's his name, I stopped for coffee near the corner of Colonus. Felt for my cell, picked out your number. The phone rang three times and the city's plague turned into a soft rain of cinnamon. I wanted you to use my ringtone, which is the Melody Maker's catchy hit, "Love Can Delay My Doom." Your message said, "I'm not here, what's your story, what's your portent. What?" I said thus: "The soup was so good, even if I couldn't see it. Let's do lunch in a dark room." I can't tell you what it meant when you called me back so soon. Your eyes, you know, let me tell the Sphinx what was what. Life, you know, is hard, when you were left to die so young. I'm glad we're going to eat.

Anna Perenna

When the past did a backflip, I remembered the circus, how they said it set out from Carthage with lots of tricks and colored cloth and animals that looked at you cross-eyed. When I was a boy, the moon moved so strangely, skimming the surface of the night skies and seeming to dip into the River Numicius. Oh, the moon, the moon, who knows why it slipped into that subtle tear in the sky and didn't come back until the healing year of acrobatic love. Now, I love wine as much as the next tumbler, and I think about a woman whose eyes could see though me, around me, and into my shoes. My soles were full of water in the morning. The branches dripped with her lemon-scented dew. She told me I would only remember her the way she prophesied until I found her refusing to bloom. "Sister, not so fast," says I. "I wouldn't cross you, but I'd be tempted to cross the river, by you. Towards Anio, from Rome."

The Stranger on K Street

I wasn't asleep and I wasn't awake. But I wanted to make things better, the way you see a door that's closed and you think it might be better open, or green, or in a little town in Belgium. If I played the guitar, I'd compose finger night music, and have my strings made by the Lovejoy Bakers. Oh, the crumbling allegros! How sweet the sugar notes. Who will taste my nocturnes? Must I find the right manhole to bring my sweets to Eurydice? Oh, dear. But where there isn't any light, there isn't any night, and my song — this song? — is a night song. Do you know any doors? Are you a sleeper, a walker?

On a Train from Ithaka to Chicago

Signs, because of the Ides, and the tidal pull of the moon, a cold eye. What does it see in me but lunacy and love, the pulling down of veils that should have covered my footprints on Paliki, and all those sorry little yards you see from your seat on Amtrak: I watch the boys and girls at play whose souls leak playfully into the ground near Syracuse.

Pearl's mother never liked me anyway. Forget Amber. Who, you ask, could forget Amber, that perfume . . . ? But Pearl was due to meet me at Alexandria. Then I read about Victor Laslzo in her damned diary.

Back on the train, I snap my fingers and say, "Dining car." It's worked in the past, hasn't it? We cross the Ormos or the Cuyahoga. This must be the place. To look in the mirror and say, "You remind me of me when I was young."

I Found It At the Movies

A song playing. Tinny. A voice singing. Thin. The wavering sun discreetly
exits. Two lovers, both in tuxes, slap their hands and dance furiously on a
soft floor, looking in each other's eyes, trying to tap. It's hard on a precipice.
Beneath them, in the valley, an arrow gets the hero in the back, just as he's
thinking it's the dark haired girl who was always true. If he could have lasted a
moment more, the jet fighter, overcoming his phobia and his family's inflated
expectations, would have fired a missile, dispersing the Indians. The blonde
who was thrown over by the dancing man in the tux gets the part, becomes a
star, solves the crime, sings the blues, finds the chalice. She marries the pilot.
They buy a record with a tinny song playing, a thin song singing. They shine a
strong light on their hands, and solve intricate mysteries with shadow puppets.
They change their last names to Charles. Things are looking up.

Down South

I got out of bed when the neon telegraph stopped. There was a white scar moving overhead, and when I flipped a coin, George Raft style, it swallowed it up like a hungry ghost. Desire before malignancy. I went to the races and saw something I thought could run at a little track at Atlanta. There was a note on my paper that said, "She'll be biting the golden apple of the sun when she comes." Instead of singing, I bet on show. It was a photo finish. Someone was whispering in my ear, arguably a feminine voice, "Come on, Arcadia." When I turned to see who it was, an outline of a woman holding a pen. I don't know who won.

Deal

In my dream Aphrodite deals. The stakes are high, but I've got a good stash. I think we're playing five card stud, but Hera says when you cut, the boys will lose their tails and I have nothing up my sleeves but little golden swallows peeking out of the edges of my fingertips. Apollo says I have a beautiful hand. Your face appears in the center of the table, like Auntie Em in the Witch's crystal ball. I feel like I have to win, which is just when Pandora puts a hand on my shoulder. She says don't look now, but the cards are almost gone. I say do I look worried, sister? I've got a wake-up call.

Late Stop

Wandering through the streets of Helios, he almost got hit by a bus. The rain was so cold each drop was like a splinter on his brow. He huddled in a doorway, lit a smoke, prayed to Athena for dry weather, for a sandwich shop close by. There was a sweet girl in gabardine showed him the way. He thought of Penny, back home in Ithaka. Forget everything you know. She'd ditched him for a smooth talker who ran numbers for the Trojans. Ham and swiss. Cup of joe. Guy sits next to him, "Mr. Telchine, who are you?" — seer type, says the problem might be history. "A love potion costs a bundle, you see, but for a dose of disenchantment, you need the big money. But I see you're a guy could use a break. Just give me everything you have." Naked and indifferent, he walked blissfully into the rain.

Harpy

She would always eat the food from my plate, take the groceries from my bag, the snacks from my pockets. But she had stunning hair — I think it transfixed me while she ate. She painted her nails a blinding color. Was it silver or mordant red? They were sharp. She pressed them into my arm. She finished my sentences before I started them. Then the music went missing from my ears. A small cut on my temple appeared, crooked like the Acheron, and a poem I had been thinking of faltered. It was about a girl who climbed a tree near Kalamiaris. She may have been a Dryad who looked across at Lesbos and wondered whether the water was cool, safe, better than oak. Gone, too, are my shoes, a lute, and a painted panel of a wolf about to devour a hare. Sometimes I can almost hear her wings. And I grow taut with an indecent paralysis: do I nail the door shut, or open it and call out?

Calypso

Calypso gave me her body in hieroglyphics. While I was thinking of Pretty Penny, Penelope in gabardine, she slipped me some pictures of herself as a tarted up Nereid in a pink dress. And there was more. I longed to leave, but there was never any wind, and when I thought of going home, she'd bury me in salt. I was no light lunch. Then she'd turn into a Cheshire Cat smile of ruby lips, full like Harlow's. O strange and irresistible synecdoche! Our kisses lasted years. But when the Fates intervened, or Zeus, or the will, and Calypso bought me that ticket for the Megabus to Ithaka, I couldn't help but wonder how long I had known that Penelope had played the part of Calypso to a fault.

Andromache

She was at her loom at the inner part of the house, weaving a double purple gown.

When an irresistible force such as you
Meets an old immovable object like me

Andromache had burnished shoulders like a languid boy warrior who could throw a spear in the day that would land in the night. But she loomed.

You can bet just as sure as you live

She exhorted her maids to set a tripod on the fire, to have a warm bath ready for Hector when the battle victorious ceased. When he came home to her.

Somethin's gotta give
Somethin's gotta give
Somethin's gotta give

Fears are the seeds of prophesy, black spots on our first blooms of desire. She heard distant cries move through the air.

When an irrepressible smile such as yours
Warms an old implacable heart such as mine

She didn't want to look, but gazing over the wall thought of a gutted ravine in Thebes.

Don't say no, because I insist
Somewhere, somehow, someone's gotta be kissed

The body of Hector, a thing, the beloved, love, now a thing, to be carried from the wall of Troy.

So, en garde, who knows what the fates might have in store?
From their vast mysterious sky?

A sound, like the Ionian sea was moving overhead towards her and coming from her heart. She would burst out the sea and her heart would kill Achilles.

I'll try hard ignorin' those lips that I adore
But how long can anyone try?

Can the dead still sip a bit of water?

Fight, fight, fight, fight, fight it with all of our might
Chances are some heavenly star-spangled night
We'll find out just as sure as we live

My orphaned boy is love. O impossible love, my stillborn child.

Somethin's gotta give
Somethin's gotta give

Your raiments I will burn. My raiments I will burn. Love does pitilessly. Dry your eyes.

Somethin's gotta give

thanks to Johnny Mercer

In Troy It Rains on Main Street

In Troy it rains on Main Street. After dark, in the window of the prosthetics shop, the pink heart suffers from an afterglow. A gallery, next door, with one photograph by Atget. Who could afford to remove it? The mist of Versailles seems like a quality of time, rather than space, making me forget the dead bodies at my feet — that one whose hand almost seems to reach for my ankle.

Fortuna

I hopped a bus for Texarkana because I had a hot date with Fortuna Primigenia. She'd booked us a room at the Motel 3, which she thought was funny because she had stayed there twice. She always thought something was going to tell us something, like the time the sky lit up from the back of that Greyhound going to Galveston, lit up like the flash of an oven in paradise, the door swinging open to something cooking that could make the world well and warm the bones of the coldest and spindliest oracle on the Panhandle. I never liked oracles much. Never liked being told which way the dirty old world was going to bounce by someone with cold eyes and a singsong voice. Thing about Fortuna, though, they were always crawling after her because she would blink and things would happen: seagulls crash into the seawall, waves rise up and bow, presidents slump over and kiss the ugly ass world goodbye. I could never even get the waitress to bring dessert. But Fortuna seemed to like me fine, liked the way I watched her, liked the way I noticed how she shifted the tides, and made armies weep. That last night at the Motel 3 was sweet and mysterious, even for Fortuna. I think what I'll remember most is her talking about those babies. How she remembered their sweetest sounds, their little soft sighs, before they quieted down. She was just starting to get dressed, pulling up her hose.

Cleveland

He had never driven through rust before, and there was nothing in his bag but a spoon with its head sawed off. Sometimes you have to drive west to get east, he realized, and sometimes you trick yourself into thinking you can walk on the waterline. The horizon is an idea, you know; you know you are, too. Why would someone have a sawed-off spoon, other than to show he could stir with anything? In a pinch. My father never showed up that night. They found the car. I dream, constantly, of him eating well.

In Dreams Begin Elsa

I wasn't that surprised by the brown paper covering the edges of the city. Sirens in the night. Toys falling like manna, at first. If the world doesn't have sharp edges what am I doing in Chinatown, shopping for pillows? Don't look now, but the liminal paint on your Band-aid is running. I turned every corner, and there was still the same old snow, making like an etch-a-sketch. How's for this: we poke a little hole and see if the car with engine running takes us to a safe house in Brooklyn, in the mountains, or that singing school for cats by the Zuiderzee. Someone clapped their hands and I sat up and thought: it's a wrap, or a joke, but is a kiss still a kiss?

My Saranyu

Saranyu can't look in a mirror anymore. Wild horses couldn't make her. Truth is, the changeling had a face like Helen, but the soul of the echoing caves of the Anathagri Hills. Splitting in two wasn't fun anymore. Each time she bent over, bent down to smell the rich earth, the seeds seemed to curdle in her mind. Running was, the sage said, an addiction. And he should know, having walked a pitted road to Vishakapatnum. Not to mention the couple of years studying with Anna Freud. After the children are loved and the husband left, after the leaves in the forest are trampled with her hooves, she still runs in the night. I watch her shyly with a hand full of grain, a hand holding the lily of the valley. She wants to be the woman she left. She wants to find the companion who will take her to a newer self. O celebrate this creature of restless yearning. O mourn this empty spirit of endless movement.

Crossing the River

If I've told you once, I've told you nine times: the coin in my mouth will be a wooden nickel. I never expected company on the journey to the darkest place. The boat can't carry two. I only hoped to forestall the departure. And did you know there's a lovely oyster bar just steps from here, with cool red leather swivel chairs, and a charming view of distant fires, where Phlegyas serves a mean Manhattan?

Pieces of a Dream

Lay before me like a broken coffee cup. On one was my mother's hand when she was five years old — it was tender and intelligent, but could hardly spell. Another: a red river with boats that looked like me. One long shard, rectangular, had the words "Missed baby blue street" in shaky script. It flew out of the room. There were others, too many to count. Who wants to count, I thought. Then, Abacus. Jim Backus. Dionysus. My father is angry, my mother lost. Magoo. Where are those glasses now? A lifetime's worth of dreams. Who but I could have broken them? This was my one great thought that day, downtown, and when I reached up to take off my hat, I realized it was not to be had.

Certain Nights

On certain nights, when the air seemed harmless, she would dress as though she were someone she knew and cook up a storm. Her hands did an arabesque over pots and pans whose flames flared and subsided, and clouds with the face of her mother times seven traced the kitchen skies over Oz. Her mother taught her how to do the twist, and put her to bed with stories of how her father had swept her off her feet. Now it's off to see the Wizard. There was a spike in the spices which, which . . . didn't click. Home is an obscene concept, she thought, stirring, looking up, thinking of Uncle Henry.

March

If you touch the walls of Troy they will not fall. The closer you come, the more you feel the echoes of old aristeias. But you're thousands of miles from Troy. I'm speaking of proximate distances. When the sword flies over your head, it blocks out the sun for just a moment. It's almost a relief. You blink before you thrust. Someone cries in a proximate distance. My legs are tired from the long march. O Achilles, was her skin as transparent as the lies I drank from my handmaid's well? When the water dried up, she suggested I listen for thunder. The proximate distance to passing storms. The last time I slept, I dreamed of a summer night, its azure sky closing down fast, each star an eye, each eye green, open, kind, coming ever so close.

Mnemosyne

Distant thunder through one open window, but the skies were as dry as her
eyes, which flashed superpowery. Mnemosynery. She looked at me over
a dirty martini and I forgot just about everything. What's she all about, I
mused, with those cute forties shoes, the herringbone glasses, and the public
weeping. After her ninth drink, she told me the weeping was a ruse. It hooked
melancholy types like me who couldn't quite steer their boats. Mnemosyne
remembered when the tin ceilings were so layered with Christmas lights that
you thought you were in the movie you always wanted to dream of a childhood
dollhouse cantina. Who could say such things and not expect you to smoke?
She uncrossed her legs. I tilted my head to increase the airflow. I remembered
— since memory seemed to be the one thing listed on every menu item, for
example:

Memory Oysters, Fresh from The First Ocean You Swam In

Coq to Think of Like the Time You Were in Marseille

Not Just Red but Erytharaen Snapper Originally Cooked by Walter de la Mare

*Sweetbreads Made According to Your Mother's Recipe. Choice of Side Dishes Made by
Your Grandmothers.*

I remembered that we had met once before. A year before? At a party in
Rhodes? She winked, or rather slowly closed one eye. "See? I've got my eye on
you, and it's got a tractor beam and a laser beam." After the requisite tender
kissing and lovemaking on the table, finally, an introduction. She said, "I'm
Juno Moneto," the Roman. Says I: "But isn't that the debased version of
Mnemosyne?" She smiled beautifully: "You asked for it, didn't you?"

Swim

The bridge has washed out.

Can I swim the Hellespont?

Love aches in my bones like a cancer of the blood.

The shoreline is my horizon, my head, a doll's head, the Gods thought would float.

Hera, let me drown and wake up with a memory like a creamy Athens sky.

My arms are broken glass. Even in the high waves I can hear everything crack.

Haemon's Song

What to do when Antigone tells you of the nights in Monte Carlo with Carlo, the boy wonder who wants to gamble her for sweetmeats. Mom, I'd hang us both in effigy, or worse, having been told to fuck off, when, roasting my heart around the campfire, the stars rain down unlucky tears. There are dead bodies over the hill. My eyes hurt. A phone is ringing inside the heart of the shepherd boy wandering in the distance. Stay out of the caves, everyone.

To Let You Know

In your dreams they sing out of tune a little, to let you know you're alive. Not even Midas can turn a trick like that, a song strung through stories, aerie and off, a joyous misperformance. In your dreams, the street where you live is cracked, to let you know about your mother's back, your father's gone. In your dreams Penelope's stockings are torn, whose ship, love? In your dreams they're singing, "Hi-de-ho," and Paris is looking at Aphrodite's fingers in the painting by Simonet. Who is he, who is she? In your dreams they're singing out of tune a little, to let you know you're alive. And you're happy, even though you're asleep.

Hard Nox

I saw Nox slip around the corner, and fell to my knees, tearing my black shirt open. I shot craps with Momus and Moros, but when Ushas strolled by in those red shoes, I thought I should call it a night. She asked me what I thought of that theory of Chaos, that love's boutique in the new svelte horizon has clothes that color your body into an ocean you can't understand. I told her to let me lick the outline of a comet, and ask her mother to turn down the lights. When things begin are the most darling questions. Let's try to write them in the sand under the dark skies covering the Aegean.

Lyssa

After the blood boils and cools, after the sky screams through itself, like
giant neighbors with thin walls and thin skins, after Heracles looks at what
he's done, and the cops come and everyone shakes their head, after the chant
of exponential pain-songs, horror movie noises that you think can kill the
virus in your heart, after you've said "you" like a pointed stick in the eye more
times than Penelope looked out her window and said, "suffocate the flowers
till morning again, trim my nails, and cut the head off another honey dove,"
after the car in the driveway has pulled away at three a.m. and the sheets
changed, after you tell me your love is a sea of lemongrass that the Gods will
only replenish with my blood, will you dress for the day, walk out into that flat
morning light that your mother blew down from the foothills, and be satisfied
with the strange silence right before the first sirens seem to whisper in the
distance?

Oracle

Jo Stafford was in a tank full of water, singing "Haunted Heart" to circling
sharks, whose hearts hardly beat at all. I didn't think this was strange, since
Delphi had turned into a Carnivale of oblique tableaus, lining the dusty streets
to the Oracle, with only a sullen burger joint or smoke shop flashing a greasy
pop of the everyday. In a tall cabinet, faced by glass, a woman in a Siren Suit,
black as the Aegean, was speaking to mice excitedly. Just down the way, a
miniature Hercules, proportionate and toy-like, was lifting himself up, first by
the arms, then by his head, a trick of gravity, or the God's good graces. Most of
the crowd, aside from Stafford, looked on at Jimmy "Spartan-buster" Franelli,
who was telling Oracle jokes on a set of ad hoc rocks. "Did you hear the one
about the time the Oracle said, "There's no time like the present?'" he said. "Guy
looks down sheepishly and tells her that one went right past me.'" I walked up
the road, determined to be told something, despite the distracting hoopla and
such. My mind was on a woman back in Thebes, and I needed to know what
she saw in herself. My Aunt Plinth said this was the secret to love, and the
Oracle at Delphi would crack the code. *You can't love an enigma, sweet boy*, that's
what the dear bird said. I walked the dusty road, past the statues with real hair
and the Boy Who Only Groaned. And the Oracle, when I got to her, told me to
have a good lunch and smoke less because desire makes us hungry, sometimes
weak, and seeing into someone else's self almost always means waiting in line
repeatedly for an answer, and even then . . .

As the Fates Would Have It

When the streetlights flash as you stroll underneath, you may think you're the source of the light. I was there, and it happened, and so it's all because of me. That's the trick of love, he thought, as Lachesis took his measure, and pointed to the screen on the building on the corner of 33rd and First. He saw a woman doing a laughing pantomime of a wilting flower and heard himself doing the voiceover, saying, "What will become of us, what will I do with you?"

Then driving down Lake Shore Drive, he thought of Leonidas, how biting your lip, you try not to taste the blood of your own self-knowledge when someone else has been told of the passage at Thermopylae. So much for trust, and Clotho wants to give me something that looks suspiciously like a mirror, but I tell her I don't know how to swim.

Apropos Atropos: what's the longest talk you've had with the dead? What's the wittiest thing they've said? If I were dead, would I need a reading light? If you brush me off, Styx and stones. I thought I saw you in my memory, forgetting you had gone, and now? The color of regret is black, the Moira say tonelessly. Dress for mourning when you forget that they kill love with a pair of scissors.

Wichita

O the Glen Campbellian melancholy of standing alone and looking out. After
a brief respite, thinking we swirled on a pretty ball, Kubrick's planetary ballet,
we learned that the earth was flat after all. Pancake theorists, in their journal,
Flat As, rejoiced by writing, "We can rest assured in the limits of curvature,"
and "Skaters will now be undeniably less paranoid." I had been listening to this
song about the flatlands for just about as far as the eye can see. And my place in
space always was predicated on needing a vacation. Love, you see, has a horizon
line. And the Wichita lineman is still on that line.

The Last Time I Saw Paris

I thought my childhood was like the aftertaste of absinthe, though I had never tasted absinthe. My friend Christine took me to a café in Montparnasse where the waitress and I thought I was amusing. I said *thank you*, instead of *yes*, which I do from time to time.

Twenty-five years ago on my birthday, I looked out the window and the radio said the Challenger fell. It rained like there was nothing doing and I heated little bottles of sake. I wondered if there was any warning. A clicking sound, a shudder. I went to an empty pub near Chalk Farm and smoked in a corner.

Paris black and white in heavy snow. Quieter than when my mother couldn't open the front door in Brooklyn because the drifts had locked us in. A Sunday in December and I was the only person leaving tracks to placate the gargoyles.

Nothing was open, or everything was open. How could I have known?

No Vertigo

Stupid, stupid, stupid. It's Midge I want. Witty sex, my funny valentine —
"Mother's here"— her voice textured like a clarinet, a counterpoint to all those
frenetic strings. Midge and me, a fly and a dog, though this is no nursery
rhyme. The heat for me has always been Midge; the real is my dream of the
impossible, not the poetic pygmalianism of Madeleine or her doppelganger:
tone deaf Judy. *Stupid, stupid, stupid.* I want Midge so we can stand in the mirror
and worship the displaced beatitudes of love. Who, after all, is losing sleep over
me? Except, of course, me. No vertigo there. Maybe a little impetigo. Keep your
glasses on, my sweet, and paint whatever your heart desires. *Smart, smart, smart.*

Big Trouble

Most of the others didn't see it coming. But tonight, I can see that everything
should have been as clear as day. Mr. G said that the tides would stop. Mr. P
said that the long curve would only fool us into slowing down and talking more.
Miss X said if the sun didn't look quite right our eyes would stop blinking and
our fingers would go slightly numb. Mr. Y said it was all in the bag if lightning
didn't turn into question marks. I was Mr. D and I said to myself today is
the day to go somewhere else, maybe pick up a bottle, think about the past.
Especially since you were balking in the shadows, miming the crash of what you
said you had wanted, something like the fossil of a dance step, more fleet than
had ever been imagined. But it never matters, how smart you think you were,
whether you saw what you heard, or couldn't take it to heart.

Something Has Happened to the Night

Something has happened to the night. It's changed. What used to be dark you can see right through. I can see you, do you see? Oh, my transparent Aspartame love, I grind my teeth and wake myself to go walking when the sun slips away.

Darkness used to be a moral song, and you walked the notes with care through streets that were as quiet as you could choose. I chose to look around and cool my heels, and always thought that around some corner some figure of a figure would move towards me with fingers glowing. A noctambulist lamenting at the same pitch as I. No hope for solace. But curable?

Every cab is driven by a ghost. Every light in the street is gas. Every time the sky flashes your father's face. Every Monday the skeleton of an unfamiliar animal. Every number a pain in your side.

Downtown a dead woman cleans the offices. Everything is spic and span. On the bridge I hear the water making like wind. A radio plays over the argument that filters through the curtains on Bushwick Avenue. How did I walk this far? Was I looking for you again?

One/Other

One says here is the bed made of glass, one says here is the black meadow. One says here is the escarpment where you fell, the other says don't look past your childhood narrows. One says your heart has just gotten into a cab. The other kisses my pill. One shows me the valley of Mingus. But I can't find the other's score. In my trembling hands, the map toward Oz has one of their tiny self-caricatures. It looks like Maria Ouspenskaya. In my back pocket, the other has slipped the train schedules for Skye, which has no trains. When I first remembered that I left my hat outside the door, one said she would burn my city and take my child away. In the final moment before the violets fell, the other said something that sounded like, "Come on," or "It's Yiddish."

I tried combining them after the first snow, after the complaints about the noise, and the silence, then the noise. But they pulled and pulled. Is that the right way one says it? Is that the right word? Is word?

One says it's because the Spring is too near. The other says it's because everything has to stop. Now.

Why Things Happen

for h.f.

There is no wind because there is no ship. There is no tree because there is no storm. On the hill a flute played a small boy, whose shoe dragged a foot along the edges of a ridge that caused the waves to spark and die. In the sky, the birds made the sun too hot to move, and a snake bit his own tail for moving too slowly. I want everything to be just as it was.

Penelope's eyes were black holes.

Peregrine

When it rained in Sicily, the boats dropped from the docks like great seals that had been slaughtered to punish time for slipping. Every man had one arrow and one oar, one to get home, one to make a woman tell her child that the sea had swallowed everything but love. But who among us was left to sit in the gardens of Troy, after those nights when the moon appeared in the shape of desire? Desire like a seed like a girl. Desire like the eyes that turn you into a water breather. Unholy desire that makes Venus punish you with desire for desire. O sea graspers, stop us before we see the gardens, they wailed, leaving only me to tell, sick with it all, and nothing to do but search for the woman who would listen and not look away with disgust.

Aletheia

... very poetic, gentlemen. Let me know when we pass the soul.
— Donald Pleasance, FANTASTIC VOYAGE

She swam inside her own body like a salmon swimming downstream. Easy, perhaps, but not quite right, moving through yourself in darkness and silence, shielded from consequence. The incredible shrinking woman, Aletheia. Where to escape, how to turn into a smaller body to enter the smaller body, an infinite regression of fluid removals until nothing is left but a vapor of selves, a suggestion of someone, little puffs of personality. Hide and be whole, she thought, swimming towards the light, which was the corner of her eye. She shed herself like a tear.

Narcissus

Here in the city, I only exist after it rains.

I start looking for myself when the thunder begins, a head start, eyes down.

Every puddle is oceanic, dear, laden with my tears of sorrow for how bitterly the world has let me slip through arcades like a low cloud.

Down by the canal, sticks are fast-healing scars on my face.

I recede in the heat; the sun, an intrusion, an invasion.

To love me is to believe that my sad surface is inviolable. To have to learn the contrary, an abomination.

As much as I deserve to love myself, only I am capable of spitting in my own face.

Melisande

My ring is in the shallows, since love is water, and I won bronze in Munich. The feeling of seaweed wrapped around your ankles is almost a cure for intimacy, so they say, when the sky trips the light fantastic. I could tell what I've seen, backstroke-wise: gills speaking of their own accord, fires that put themselves out for fear of rain, undersea caves where you meet the shadow of what you want, shake its liquid hand, and agree to part as friends, but not really. Last night, when I woke, a dream followed me down the stairs like the ghost of a dolphin. The sound it made had the uncanny echo of Jackie Wilson from a third floor window of an apartment near Venice Beach. Inside the apparition were two swimmers, drifting apart. One seemed to be crying, but in water who can tell?

Ricochet Avec Soleil

You look into her eyes and see the reflection of yourself turning a corner, heading down a blind alley. Later, looking out a window at a window, you see the reflection of a plane briefly flicker past. You're both headed in the same direction, you think. Indonesia. Unless you're seeing things.

You're seeing things. Has it ever made a difference? Why ask? Why not ask? Or why ask now?

The Code

I won't, because all of me wants to regardless of consequences...
— Humphrey Bogart as Sam Spade, Maltese Falcon

that Ephialtes of Trachis will be sitting by your door, his hand in his mouth, whimpering

that Xerxes will wrap you in muslin, laughing at a smile like the Anopea pass; He loves to pretend he has a traitorous tongue

that I'll fall on the sword of my own self-duplicity, love was a small city made of ash that I built in the basement

that the clocks will run backwards on the symmetrical day of the month, in homage to the essential grotesqueness of simple math; no one should attempt to add to himself

that under the el I'll always notice that water drips and never find out why — I'll hear that dripping sound, always

that when you fight a sacred war, for twenty-five dollars a day (plus expenses) the Persians may admire you up to a point, and the Greeks think you're an upstanding fellow for not ducking out, but you'll always have that bullseye on my heart, or on my back

See Patroclus

When an airplane crashes in a room in a dream, there is hardly any room for
time. You try to move the chairs, the cupboard. You think of getting out of the
way. And then you look over and see Patroclus, whom you love. His sword is
out, but the jet is skidding over the parquet floor. Fifty-three men fell for him.
The engines roar. The emergency slides deploy. Your mother's favorite teacup,
the one with china roses up to the lip, is in pieces at your feet. You take the
sharpest piece, run it over your tongue, wake with blood on the pillow.

Les Oiseaux de Paris

All the birds of Paris are sick. The herring gull skulks along the Seine like Mistinguett with her vocal cords cut. I saw her do this once on stage, opening and closing her beak, a c-flat or two floating yawning sideways to the boxes. Swan song. The mute swan, though, is especially mute, not wanting, I think, to become Odette again. Instead, Odette will head to *Swann's Way*. And Siegfried can have his idyll alone.

A rock dove swings wildly from a gargoyle, mourning a honey dove. O the melancholy, melodramatic birds of Paris. They're sick. They won't last the night. Only you and I see the rock dove as he falls.

And there, near an arcade, perhaps the Vivienne, there are silhouettes on the ground—ghosts of the last starlings in the arrondissement. They started to appear all over Paris the night your words turned black and grew wings. *Don't worry*, you told me, *they're blackbird words*. But all that nocturnal talking and buzzing, all those empty skies clued me in. Those words were carrion crows, here to stay.

In Place

I know your mild dissatisfaction was sincere, when you were kissing your lover's
thigh, there, in Crete, while the sky turned to chalk and a mad centaur raked
his bloody cock on a nearby tree. That a Manticore dragged a girl with curly
hair away to his cave screaming was, you must admit, unfortunate. When she
emerged, her hands weltered in gore, the upgraded ticket for the Metroliner was
a lovely gesture, but I think you could have at least read her a bedtime story.
You see, nothing is meant to survive the movement into that darkness. When it
does, best to make something up. Pour a stiff one. Pray.

Who's Afraid of Helen of Troy

If I hear you once more say the word *love*, I'll take the imaginary child, his hair gleaming on my shield, or reflected in your Suburu's window, and present him on a platinum platter for the Cyclops to devour for the world's amusement. This is commensurate with the nature of my powers and the natural state of a healthy relationship, not to mention the good of the polity. There is a jigger of brandy on the sideboard, if you like. And I hear a Sirk is playing at the Odeon. Most of the army has been ripped apart on the plain, and merely waits for the pyres. But a plate of sandwiches and some civil conversation would be the least one could expect after all we've meant to each other. Through the bluish muslin curtains, I can hear someone whisper you can see the sails on fire. Like floating fireworks, or flashes in the eye. Let's talk about the future, or futures, life as a commodity. Let's fall on the sword of a memory of chance. Let's put on a record of Noel Coward. Let's dance.

Killing a Rock with a Spider

Grab the spider firmly with your hand, keeping some distance from the rock. Superstition says you shouldn't kill a rock, but all the prophets have been thrown from the cliffs, their bodies defiled, their tax schemes exposed. Lift your hand high, and don't squeeze too tightly, or look directly at the sun or moon — the former, for your eyes, the latter for the chilly dance you did that lunar equinox on the heath, a kind of saunter, childish, flapping wings — it would make you do unspeakable things if you remembered it too soon. Too soon or ever. Now, or in a dream . . . Bring down the spider as hard as you can. See what you've done. Calmly walk away.

Questions for The Sphinx

Are you sad that the riddle is considered a debased form, having been the genre of life and death?

When you asked about my mother, why were your claws out?

Are your lips as soft as your tail is long?

So you don't think it's rude to answer a question with a question?

Did you know I was coming? Were the other answers funny, or a bore?

Does the connection, etymologically, to sphincter, embarrass you or excite you?

When you threw the others over, or ripped them up, did you smile your Mona Lisa smile, like now, or ever feel a moment of remorse?

If I were to sing "Night and Day," would a purr rise in your throat? Could I touch your sharp teeth while you dreamed?

Did you ever think of destroying Thebes and protecting the men who came to you with no answers?

Is there a nice inexpensive place to eat around here? I'm supposed to dine with mother.

Five Unscrambled Anagrams

Not her mother's lost rage.

Love's cave buried platitude.

Cowardly nocturne shirking desire.

Yarn fingers busy mourning.

Trusting words bite head off.

Let's Go to Troy

apologies to Cole Porter

We might have been meant for others
But the Gods' opposition, can stoke not smother
This feeling, yes a feeling, it's called a feeling, unconcealed
It's neurotic, clearly sclerotic, full of feelings that are congealed

Darling, if you feel as well about the hell we can have once more
Love's simulacrum is a fancy candy store
Which serves my fevered nerves
With the sugar from your fulsome words

Let's go to Troy, why shouldn't we go to Troy
We'll make a trip of it, get good grip on it
We'll go to Troy

Swords near our thighs, no price is ever too high
Ready to thrust them then, don't trust the other men
We'll watch them die

Let's make believe that there's a chance for relief
And the ways we danced on the grave of joy was a lark
We might have been meant for others
But the Gods' opposition can stoke not smother

Let's go to Troy, why shouldn't we go to Troy
Time's wasted anyway, we're not so young
Let's go to Troy

Acknowledgements

Many thanks to the editors of the following journals where these prose poems first appeared.

Sundog Lit, special issue, Letters From the Road: "Cleveland" and "Ricochet Avec Soleil," Fall 2014.

DMQ Review: prose poems, "Anna Perenna," "Lyssa," and "Peregrine," Summer 2014.

Rhino: "Why Things Happen," prose poem, Spring 2014

TriQuarterly: "Who's Afraid of Helen of Troy," Summer 2014.

Tusculum Review: prose poem, "The Last Time I Saw Paris," Spring 2014.

Denver Quarterly: "The Stranger on K Street," and "At a Diner Near Thebes," Summer 2012.

The Laurel Review: "Haemon's Song," "Hard Nox," and "Fortuna," Summer 2012.

Malpais Review, Special Noir Section: "Late Stop," "In Dreams Begin Elsa," forthcoming Fall 2012.

Books from Etruscan Press

Zarathustra Must Die | Dorian Alexander
The Disappearance of Seth | Kazim Ali
Drift Ice | Jennifer Atkinson
Crow Man | Tom Bailey
Coronology | Claire Bateman
What We Ask of Flesh | Remica L. Bingham
The Greatest Jewish-American Lover in Hungarian History
      Michael Blumenthal
No Hurry | Michael Blumenthal
Choir of the Wells | Bruce Bond
Cinder | Bruce Bond
The Other Sky | Bruce Bond and Aron Wiesenfeld
Peal | Bruce Bond
Poems and Their Making: A Conversation | Moderated by Philip Brady
Crave: Sojourn of a Hungry Soul | Laurie Jean Cannady
Toucans in the Arctic | Scott Coffel
Body of a Dancer | Renée E. D'Aoust
Scything Grace | Sean Thomas Dougherty
Surrendering Oz | Bonnie Friedman
Nahoonkara | Peter Grandbois
Confessions of Doc Williams & Other Poems | William Heyen
The Football Corporations | William Heyen
A Poetics of Hiroshima | William Heyen
Shoah Train | William Heyen
September 11, 2001: American Writers Respond | Edited by William Heyen
American Anger: An Evidentiary | H. L. Hix
As Easy As Lying | H. L. Hix
As Much As, If Not More Than | H. L. Hix
Chromatic | H. L. Hix
First Fire, Then Birds | H. L. Hix
God Bless | H. L. Hix

Etruscan Press Is Proud of Support Received From

Wilkes University

Youngstown State University

The Ohio Arts Council

The Stephen & Jeryl Oristaglio Foundation

The Nathalie & James Andrews Foundation

The National Endowment for the Arts

The Ruth H. Beecher Foundation

The Bates-Manzano Fund

The New Mexico Community Foundation

Drs. Barbara Brothers & Gratia Murphy Endowment

The Rayen Foundation

The Pella Foundation

Founded in 2001 with a generous grant from the Oristaglio Foundation, Etruscan Press is a nonprofit cooperative of poets and writers working to produce and promote books that nurture the dialogue among genres, achieve a distinctive voice, and reshape the literary and cultural histories of which we are a part.

etruscan press
www.etruscanpress.org

Etruscan Press books may be ordered from

Consortium Book Sales and Distribution
800.283.3572
www.cbsd.com

Small Press Distribution
800.869.7553
www.spdbooks.org

Etruscan Press is a 501(c)(3) nonprofit organization.
Contributions to Etruscan Press are tax deductible
as allowed under applicable law.
For more information, a prospectus,
or to order one of our titles,
contact us at books@etruscanpress.org.